Out of Bounds

Scripta Humanistica

Directed by
BRUNO M. DAMIANI
The Catholic University of America

ADVISORY BOARD

Out of Bounds

Elizabeth Sullam

Scripta humanistica

35

Elizabeth Sullam,
    Out of Bounds

    (Scripta humanistica; 35)
    I. Title. II. Series: Scripta Humanistica
(Series); 35.
PR9120.9.S809   1987   821   87-12822
ISBN 0-916379-40-X

                          Publisher and Distributor:
                          SCRIPTA HUMANISTICA
                            1383 Kersey Lane
                        Potomac, Maryland 20854 U.S.A.

                     Printed in the United States of America

For the Dead of All Wars

"Father forgive them; for they know
not what they do."

Jesus Christ

Luke 24, 34

This book is also dedicated to my son, Federico Augusto whom I love above all, and who by hook or by crook stood always beside me.

Acknowledgments

Very special appreciation to Shirley Cochrane, Mary Ann Larkin, Chris Llewellyn, who have inspired, guided, and supported me in more ways than one.

Thanks to Elisavietta Ritchie, who included me in her "Macomb Street Group" and gave valuable advice; to Bradley Strahan, who helped with belief and encouragement; and to Elizabeth Ford, who provided me with her short course in poetry.

To my dear Gabriele Glang, and Carolyn Kurylo, fine poets and friends, I owe a great debt for their sensible and aesthetic comments. My gratitude goes also to Sharon Costello, Stacy Tuthill, Atanas Slavov, as well as to Alicia de Joux, who gave some order to chaos.

Betty Parry assisted me with her coaching, and especially love. She is a rare person to me. I thank also Richard Harteis, much admired poet and human being for a very enlightening afternoon, and William Meredith, whose eyes speak more than words.

A special place in my heart is reserved to the Indreeides of Norway; Erling, excellent poet, for his impeccable suggestions; Kirsti, his wife, a lady of true Renaissance spirit and much loved; their children: Carl Christian, the young music critic; Bendig (my pet), the scientist; and Oslak, of the big eyes, who understands English more than anyone may think, "Thanks for listening to my reading my nocturnal long chatting, but above all for company and love."

To my dearest friends of many years, Marifrances and O. B. Hardison I am especially indebted for their enduring friendship, support, valuable counseling. To O.B. my gratitude for reading the manuscript and expressing his much valued opinion. "Your letter, dear friend, moved me very much and I am enriched by your words."

I single out Jean Nordhaus, whose excellent work created special resonance in my world, and who contributed new insights, perspectives, special sensibility; and Katherine Zadravec, who in critical times extended herself enormously to give me her unerring judgment.

To Jean, Catherine, and O.B. I can only say: "Without your help I would not have dared." To May Miller and Elaine Magarrell profound thanks for their encouragement and time.

To Dr. Joseph Harmon of Chicago I owe a great deal: his criticism has changed my writing dramatically.

My heartfelt "grazie" to Dr. Lee Eiden, my friend for a long time, and his wife, Marybeth, who has been most gracious, patient, and supportive. Lee not only assisted me in editing, gave me fresh ideas, erased inconsistencies, but also helped in the technical preparation of the manuscript.

I express my appreciation to Frances Brown, who typed the first draft.

To the countless persons whom I may have failed to mention for the sake of brevity go my apologies and fondest appreciation.

Some of these poems have been published by: *Di Versi in Versi*, Parma, Italy; *Federal Poets*, Washington, D.C.; *Gargoyle*, Washington, D.C.; *Lip Service*, Washington, D.C.; "American Classic" and "The Cooke Book," Scop Publications, College Park, Md.; *Visions*, Arlington, Va.; Wineberry Press, Washington, D.C.

Foreword

Here is poetry, with the heft that comes from a gift for catching in flight a particular person, a place, an event, an object: a Bolognese beggar with St. Vitus' dance, for example, or a grandmother's jewelled egg that "sorrows for passing glances/in some aseptic museum." The vivid registerings of what is singular repeatedly tempt the eye, like floats in a passing parade. But Elizabeth Sullam is also searching for, and soon enough searching through what is permanent.

Again and again in these poems the preoccupied moment glides, or leaps, or sinks into a larger matrix. One finds impulses of personality sewn, with strokes both deft and solicitous, through an unfolding fabric of time. The image of rivers, in "Confluence," blends stability and surprise in the lives of two women ("no matter how middle-aged") forming a fast friendship:

> Our religion is the law of flowing,
> our temptation is the plain, our sin is
> outflowing, our redemption receding,
> our interdict the rock, our passion the sea.

Eventually, as in "Lights at Romsdal," the poetry reaches out to revise creation, where the light is "too much...to bear,"

> as if the air, bare peaks and waterfalls
> cried for it and an incontinent god
> complied.

In that divine admixture of compliance and incontinence something basic to Elizabeth Sullam's imagination discloses itself. Her work gives evidence of one too gracious, too wise not to be compliant (also too subtle not to show, as in the recurrent passages on woman's experience, how poignant and galling compliance can be). The poems also show an inherent power not to be contained in standard forms and responses. Crafted, accumulated through silent decades that Horace, the preacher against hurrying to print, would sagely approve, they come before us now as winning and telling forms of

> The speech of things! and their craving for
>   existence!
> Things solving enigmas, things familiar,
>   expansive, urgent, processing their holders,
>   welding ceaselessly,
> like damned blacksmiths, distance to distance,
>   link after link....

The poems pause, once, to ask the reader: "how did you bear up/in foreign traffic?" They themselves bear up more than passing well.

Michael G. Cooke
Professor of English
Yale University

TABLE OF CONTENTS

III. Quarrel with Death

IV. Miserere

V. At the Edge of the Land

Landscape

Lugano

The one o'clock is late.
Wrapped in cold sun, furs and coats,
few huddle here to tour the lake:
my mother, ninety, from Milan;
I from America;
two damp German couples,
efficiently gemütlich;
brother and sister,
Bostonian, politely aloof;
two Japanese businessmen;
a Dutch engineer.

The dock becomes a stage
mother holds against
the slackness of the season
and the services,
and when the Germans give her their fat support
and spread their hands
upon the printed schedule,
she shares with them
the name of her summer retreat.

How well she plays her part...
she, who on our way
had asked me, suddenly,
"What do you think one feels
in dying?"

Between the polished benches of the boat,
her question seems to float among us,
strangers,
and among the swans and mallards
that quiver at the lake edge.
It lingers for me in her brown eyes.

Like windows of houses empty in winter
my words shut down inside me.
A habit of silence,
grown between us,
keeps them locked away.

Beyond seagulls, dock polers, signs,
my silence scans the farther lake
of oleanders, cypresses and pines,
wending along villages, villas,
rests on leafless branches
shaking on the steel grid
of light-touched waters.

Mother, I am sad, confused,
my future, like your own,
casts a stunted shadow.
I, too, am close to the other side
where shrubs grip the dust
of crumbling slopes.

August 4, 1983

I cannot tell why memory
feeds upon secret wells
where desires are not dead but sleep
and leap at the strangest summons.

Blue swells flowing on the frail
hands of a Russian emigré
call to mind your long slender hand
offering Fräulein Elizabeth and me
Heller candies in the Prater

or leaves' slow pattering
behind my shoulders
are ever your soft laughter
at a Mantua circus, reassuring me
frightened by a clown.

A long farewell lingers
between you and me, Father,
an unfinished gesture, lifting a curtain
over a desolate inner landscape

where your image seems held back,
color thinned, outlines distorted
fragments fleeting in an insubstantial
medium. I have grown accustomed
to your fading away, and the seeming peace
of not being certain what we were
or if we were at all, outside of one another.

Today you would be eighty-six.
There is in my well a falling
of evergreens, lichens, mosses—
in my landscape a surf of shadows.

Beggar with Saint Vitus' Dance

Every morning
they left you
to earn a few "centesimi"
against the last column
of the arcade
on the left arm
of the crossroads
opposite our school.

A thin man,
jerking and shaking,
dancing his endless dance
—kite
in a stormy sky.

And we, healthy,
young, rushing
our fretful revulsion
about you,
throwing our alms
with lowered eyes
in the tin can
lying at your feet.

I, guilty, shy,
scared
until one day,
by chance,
looked into your eyes,
steady
in all that twitching flesh.

Gentle eyes,
nazarene-brown,
cried out
the yearning
of your soul—ship
anchored
to so forsaken port,—
sang
the song your voice
could not sing.

We knew, we knew,
precarious beggar,
and we became then
two binary stars.
You a huge red giant
pulsating your solitude
on the most solitary province
of a little star
that fired into brilliance.

And now,
empty of myself,
I have returned to your corner,
empty of you,
but still pulsating.

Around,
aimless Bologna
still rushes,
empty
of her center,
empty
of her medieval mind,
and dark
as the old canal
now flowing beneath asphalt,
darker
than the ancient university's
sable courtyard.

Where are you, precarious
proscript?
Where storms cease
and there are no alms?
Where
finally motionless
finally calm
you may intone
your first free song?

Caretaker

Grandmother bestowed on me
her lore and wisdom of wifehood—
Charm. Please. Obey.
Give him male children.
Make the home one he will
come back to. Mistresses
for men are a way of life,
never to be noticed or discussed.
Discretion
the keystone to matrimony.

My father, the Sun God,
showered on me
his dismissing rays:
"A woman must give.
Persevere. Her husband will take care
of her patrimony, her welfare." How could I fail?

By night you called me Ino, Aspasia, Madame
Pompadour. In daylight, Gaspara, Hypatia,
Madame de Staël, Victoria. I responded.
Between calls, I remodeled the house,
pacified cooks, butlers, gentleman's gentlemen.
Our first child was christened with your father's
name. In the garden I planted birds of paradise;
started bonsai in the greenhouse. Ignored
your mistress, knowing looks of friends.

Had I misheard you? Old names no longer suited.
You were praising daredevils, explorers, aviators.
"Amelia help me!" I tried to defy gravity.
My wings too small, I dangled in mid-air.
Dared even more: disguised as Fangio, I took
my chances at Monza, Monte Carlo, the Carrera.
You roared by me, blind-armored in your red
Maserati. Our second child was named after
your mother. The butler left. You got
a British one, and a new mistress, younger,
more athletic.

Grandmother suggested: "Penelope...perhaps..."
I wove patiently at polo games.
Spun at Ascot, the Harris Bar. Smiled at suitors'
jokes. Waving my veil I sidestepped their passes
at charity balls. By the time I cut my hair short,
tinted it ash blond, you had diverted from Cairo
to Mombasa, a gorgeous Spanish creature, raven black.

The chameleon longs to take the color of the earth;
listens to no other voice except its own.
I returned home. Still, for a while, I kept
a wishbone in my bag. For years now,
among races, polo, mistresses—younger and younger
and more defiant—you have come in and out
of home, sure of your names, master, caretaker,
playboy, lover, etc. You've never seen my heart
beating on the Aubusson, my arms and legs
stone-lonely on the four-poster bed, never known
that when you called me, I touched down
on bayonet-meadows, where your calls flew
on monkshood wings, your poppy red beak
tore off whatever name you gave me.

You keep naming me, certain of your game of the name.
You haven't even noticed I've collected my heart,
my limbs, bonsai, birds of paradise, and gone
to live, unfaithfully, elsewhere.

Chiaroscuri

Come winter we converged in Arles,
You from the North, I from the South.
Locked in desire, we barred all we left
behind, and the vast sweep of peace of the
Camargue raised a discreet screen between
two alone and the proud tides outside.

Now for twelve solitary years I, like a teal,
have come here seeking sanctuary where dusk draws
fog in its wake, tailing the long flight
of flamingoes, stretched like a flame toward
some remote retreat. Meres and marshes
and shallow waters glimmer, darken, and speak
your lost name with one liquid voice.

Today *chiaroscuri* are shifting over the Vaccarés.
Secluded on my stump of dune, I see a fluid
world narrow and assume a molten face. Fogfolds
moving at a slow pace grow grayer in patches.
One patch latches another. Afar, a fogbow glimmers
translucent through the hooded eye of the sky.

A reluctance surges, unforeseen, against the oldness
of my dream, against the familiar foam and gray waters.
An urgency of salt comes from the breath of the fighting
sea to my shoulders, perhaps oppressed by the bitter
burden of the old hurt. A frenzy frets from the mouth
of the delta and opens the land to the sea.

13

The fogbow, now near, aglow over the slate colored fleece
of the fog, like an alabaster bowl, yields light
and new offerings. Life, awakened, avid, flickers
like a fresh fire and whips the passion of the Northern
wind.
The bittern breaks the black confines of your night
with deep conch calls. The safe veil of dreaming falls,
my love. I fear what lies beyond the gray lines of the reef.

Charterhouse of Maggiano

The Sienese countryside has not crumbled
since we drove through this restricted landscape
of short flattened waves, olive-crested,
cypress-rippled.
The Charterhouse we visited in ruins
has been transformed into a five-star hotel.
From three windows in my tower room
a deeper shade of brown, cropped, winter earth
rolls to walled roads. Is it you there
emerging on your way back from an early hike?

Last night in the old library (now game room
and bar), a sheik, incongruous in tuxedo,
teaching backgammon to his Swiss girlfriend,
grinned at me. From across the table
your smile flashed, boring through the dull pain
embedded in my heart.
All night you keep me awake. Sketched by dimness
your face looks unbearably young. I hope
you do not notice the furrows cut in mine.

In the cloister you stand upright, staring,
beneath the crescent of an Italian Gothic arch.
Your cigarette swishes like a solitary firefly.
I say softly: "Please John, don't smoke so much,"
and wait for you to answer, "Don't worry, love,
one of these days I'll stop."

I know, I know, at night this place possesses us,
keeping our season of joy awakened within these
walls, and safe from the chimeras of day,
from the fire they swivel at noon around the vague
convolutions of ironworks on top of the well's
ring of serena stone. Will we be here unchanged,
unchangeable forever, as we have been for ages
since we called this abbey sanctuary?

Rose hints the consciousness of dawn.
The aubade of one sparrow wakens the roof's
menagerie, the cats in the cloister,
the belfry bells. Night shapes, known only to me
at the windows of my room, slide away,
one feeding on the other, like the drops
along the black balcony rail—one reaching,
the next fleeing to splash on the courtyard's
patterned tiles. Your shape lingers awhile.
I try to touch the curve of your lips,
and cannot reach. The fast turning
violence of the sun uncolors us,
the abbey, the chimera, the sky.

"The Deep Heart's Core"

No matter whether life
came into being
just as it is now,
or through an elaborate selection,
whether time is linear or circular.
The problem is that to get
him or her who is responsible
is like trying to catch a fish
with bare hands.
Apparently God, because a couple—
probably hungry—ate an apple
from his or her orchard, decided
to withdraw and make things
very difficult for the two culprits
and their progeny as well.
At the heart of the plum: all the officially recognized
retainers of the truth
call their sundry gods amiable,
merciful, and just.
That's really amazing.
So, they had to discover the snake.

Eris

We ask questions we can answer no more.
If we spoke words would have other meanings,
or none at all. Our eyes sent messages of frost,
their cold syllables slivered on our skin
long before they found their way to sound.

The hall mirror reveals two masks of *papier maché*,
withered roses brim over a dry vase.
After you have slammed the door, a voice,
not yet mine, asks whether there were ever faces
beneath the masks.

Leaving

It was hard to leave the house,
the misty river and stones
that hold so much of one
and those who came before,
and made all bear their space,
their heaviness and air.

To open gates, tear down walls,
go outside and understand
the winds of the plains;
to reach the river mouths and feel
what rivers feel when
their sweet waters meet
the salty waters of the sea;
to cross straits, be at the merge
of sea with ocean; stand where
oceans, drinking distant sands
and rocks, are drunk by them;
to follow spice routes and
the bargaining of souls and gods;
learn the tongue of tongues,
and seek the bluest flower.
This is an act that must be done
to reconcile that part of one
that wants to be what one is not
and free.

Breaking loose—
only to feel the stones have grown
heavier on one's shoulders, wells deepened,
and find winds blow only
silence on the plains,
oceans swallow sweet waters
and drown seafarers;
great routes crumble into ruins;
spices dry and souls are sold into slavery;
gods fight over nothing;
blue flowers do not bloom;
and one is always crouched
in secret gardens,
watching the same fountains,
where the nightingale
is mad with night,
and blood with jasmine and nightshade,
where one grows to be
what one becomes.

You No Longer Sail the Boat

She lies upon the shore
of our pine-walled cove.
The current steers, at whim,
the helm unlashed,
the hull long thrashed
by wind and wave, the name washed out.
You no longer name me mate.

At night, at the Casino,
the roulette wheel
swivels against my bet.
No more chips are left.
You don't sound out the spinnings,
other games lure you, dark
games I don't yet know.

You don't see me returning to the dock.
The breakers churn and foam. Our boat
surges, like a figment of herself,
chiseled, waiting
against the flares of the sky,
and does not know my coming and going.

The footsteps sandaled
in the needles of the sloping lane
through the pine grove, sag into silence

and here, in the last slice of my evening
listening for your laughter,
I hear only the sea.

Exile

This place is transparent and null
as a heap of dragonfly wings
at the end of summer. My house
has been built at a new world's edge
where spindrift whitens the air.

In the empty conch of evening
winds play grand themes
of absence, in flat phrases without rest,
familiar now to my ears as the song
of strange birds on my sill.

In my garden, night's fluid
thickens with alien spices,
wild honey from quiet beehives—
the stars a shiver of lace
on the skin of the sky.

The Hydra of morning; tentacles of water
wash away my footsteps. The same sea-monster,
a single wave that floods two shores—a single lamentation
uttered by two lips. No sadder sound
was ever heard or carried
over Earth's wide spaces.
My land, see how the oil lamp
under the roof of our dreams
is shaking.

Memory-house

As I left, I turned to look. I saw you
fastened to the Padusian plain, filled
with time at the edge of the wind's domain.
Emptiness passed through your windows, portals,
walls, merged with the stillness in the sky,
closed in, one, into my shrunken heart.
Suddenly the sun flooded from clouds,
and you threw your strength into my eyes.
View landscaped for the soul between two presences
of sky, one in the moat, one above, you stood
a full statement with a single word: endure.

That pure sound, now mine and purer,
repeated in many halls of time and space,
against the world's other face, where the sea
rages, and no one plants rosemary at the doorside,
and elms fade like fragrance on sick skin.

Parent, cradle, mentor, master. I endured,
a part of you. From afar you beaconed the vistas
of our landscape, sang their windswept songs:
the dull plon-plon of the watermelon barges
slow-moving
on the river, the sprung rhythm
of the story-teller in the fountained square,
the angry rice-picker women's chants. I relived
the blue immobility of the sky, the green
undulation of the grass, the low clouds
swarming like runaway thoughts of youth,
moon's unceasing foundering of night,
night untying the moorings of the stars,
black brilliance far beyond the reach of eyes.
I savored the safe flavor of morning baked bread,
the stench of wet hemp, the sweet pungency
of walled gardens, the scent of autumn rains.

I never despaired. The raging sea grew calm,
grape clusters glowed in deserts, words of mercy
rang like church bells amid unlawful crowds.
Flagstone-base of towers, carrying their height,
defying erosion, your limber language,
in the ternary rhythm of its greatest poet,
carved the first images of my mind. Proceeding
out of itself, it lifted me above the past,
above new forces, and the rifts of years to come
which men now have already begun to live; and alerted me
to see as one our voices and the voice of alien speech.

Once more, walking on the beach of a new land,
I wait, like the shore, for an eyeblink of tides,
when waves wash breezes of fire. One phantom,
memory and you, house. So come again,
and like the sea grown calm, let ripples
shine. Shower me with the pearls of your splendor
before the dark face of Janus claims us.

"Garda See"

Slowly the car cliffs down
the spit of land. The cypress lane
bends only once now. There is no trace
of the wild rose or oleander vases.
The entryway is paved. Flecks
of cyclamens on the undulating meadow
write the slender quest
of an old slow-turning world
against fast spreading concrete and steel.
What myths will be still moored
to the small dock on the cove,
what murmurs will loom
inside the villa, I do not know.
One tends to be literary in letters;
the face of yesterday hardens into forms.
I feel fear will make me tell
the driver to turn back, but
a slim silhouette darts from the shade
of the Doric colonnade;
a hand piercing through the hoary
ferns of my mind scribbles a smile
on my lips. "Princess"—the old
nickname shakes my breast.
"Gypsy"—Bona ties me into embrace—
"You are finally back."

Sparks of young laughter
fill up spaces between columns;
memories light each Murano chandelier;
room after room glitters.
Dreams that never took place
come dancing to waltz with us
among odors of tea, amber
of champagne. They come through the clear
autumn air, along the lane, upon the dock,
upon ourselves, girls again, one again
with the cobalt imagination of the lake.

Stay

What I have not seen long since, I find again
along the shortcut, rocky as it climbs,
easy when it downs to the copse and meadow
of the old family home. Between autumn and winter
when all chestnuts, swollen, have already fallen
and rain and hunts have passed,
the sky intimates, and the land
prepares for the chill, pure light of snow which
soon will shawl the turf and warm the seeds.

It is near evening, and the fog, pliable,
tepid with the breath of stables, milk,
and peaceful sleep, fills the fields; smoke
puffs over the blush of steep roofs
and hazel tufts. Strange silence and solitude
take hold of the cold garden meadow
as when long ago, before dinner, all of us
stepped out from the warm hall to stroll
into nipping dusk. There was no sound
but the soft trust of my people's
voice. It comes back now, softer,
more remote, yet insistent, as the fall
of water from the distant fountain spout—
a human calling strewn with bare boughs,
stiff fir cones, the nettle creepers,
the unpruned shrubs. Stay, stay close—
the voices say—Here is your grail
guarded by the gargoyles of the Lombard church
steady through centuries on her knoll of marble.

29

Here the hazel, walnut, the chestnut trees live
their seasons free. The Hippogriff finds its moon.
Rinaldo, Angelica, Medoro ride the long crest
of the riverbanks, and Roland which his Durendal
keeps at bay the monsters which try to grab
the flatland. Still the sky sketches the stories
of Andromeda, Orion, and the Centaurs,
and the small bank exchanges your old coins.
In the library, dust has not settled upon
Pliny, the Divine Comedy, Paradise Lost...

O stay close to the earth where your seed
first sprouted. Here your roots reach deep.
Here your day detaches itself from toil,
and your soul's turmoil is hushed by the fog.
Hear the last cry of the coots, coping
the village roofs.

Night Walks Unaware

of her own doings
over the gypsy chants
that make each hour grow old
as the accompanying sea.
The campfires graze the threshold
of the hill and strike their light
along the grove and massive wall shadow,
like the tendrils of the trumpet
creeper you planted. They coil around,
reverse, rebind to an old stump
and give it the semblance of vigor.

Nearly all our friends are gone,
like you, *amico mio*. Fewer and fewer
things are certain now, and one by one
the tokens are withdrawn
from a world growing ugly and unholy
in the hands of merchants, barbarian swarms
from within and out.

Our perched town, our castle,
stand lone, lofty, aloof,
incomprehensible as the words
I use to describe them to the paying
multitudes who come to visit. Even children
and grandchildren of our friends
do not understand, or care to.

31

I think I see your eyebrows arch
slightly, a surprised smile
curve upwards the corners of your lips
when a woman wearing red tights
exclaims, looking at your portrait:
"What a hunk, look Mary, what a hunk!"

Night mends all ugliness
and out of it emerge the forms
I am accustomed to, spiralling
intermittently into view,
filling the redeeming stillness,
as the old clock
fills the drawing room with minutes
already gone, or the single pine
the space of the once thriving forest.

The Sap of Oleander Thickened in Your Veins

A universe began to constrict
long ago on Rialto Bridge.
Sap of oleander thickened in your veins.

The jackal god kept watch on our doorsteps.
It has followed the ambulance,
run with white uniforms along
rainbowed tracks, toward the non-human
sounds from your lungs.
Now its muzzle sniffs Lysol and the wires
connecting you with the pump.
Its lapis lazuli eyes close on my vigil.
In the sky Lucifer is a neon cross.

Are you waiting with me for the opening
of the narrowest door?
Nothingness will have your face
and the voice of your doctor.
It has already diffused
in the drugged brightness of your eyes,
in the resentful flow of my blood.

The downward zig-zag line
on the puzzle page of the *New York Times,*
when the pencil slipped from your hand;
the icy beeps and buzzes of the monitor
have prepared me for the last continuous shriek.

33

When the shriek scatters the August afternoon
pomegranates burst on Key Bridge.
On the windowpane a stranger's face
stares back at me. A dumb scream
begins to uncoil on the tongue of Anubis.

Something Flowering

In Sevilla

All signs erased from the sky, a moonthick surf
hurls me between the pale matter of its tides.
There is no dreaming, but the snake-belly
tightening and swelling of hours. Venus' brittle
luster dies and dies in the meadow of my eyes.
A few low stars break into whisper. Is it time?
Is my dark substance sliding toward decline?

Just when this Walpurgis night seems
never to end, chaste clouds filter a foam of white
that falls upon the frozen flight of hills;
behind trails a red-yellow bow of light
and dark recedes west of the Guadalquivir.
Below the edge of my garden steep, green manes
hang from the sky half dark, half light; trunks
and roots lie asleep with the secret valley, deep
in a sea of mist slow-curling and dissolving.

My thoughts, released from the hard confines of dark,
run up the slope hungry for warmth like strayed
garden cats. Something flowers immense, sheer,
above crests, boulders, olive groves.
In the now clear valley the river responds
glitter to glitter. Sevilla lifts her fingers
to the sky, to bless another day and me, surprised
to be in it, surprised by butterflies that wing
a paper-prayer in the November wind—to flutter
a little longer over this ocher earth, taste
the cactus flower—Would that I could
stretch this hour as far as the last
bright-tailed star that lights my hill
and the next hill, and more, and more, and more...

Return to "El Almendral"

I have been drawn here by nights of nightingales,
day gray glow of olive groves, falls of jasmine
and bougainvillea on the rim of brain.

The Spanish sky, starry-deep, still holding
its charts of joy and grief, is flung
wide by fuller moons that give the land
a mood of brown sea surface and hermit peace.

I walk my sleepless way to the *orangerie*.
My eyes, my skin catch in each shadow
of the patio palms and the tiles'
sheen that seems more brilliant
as it sharpens to silver.

Moonlight, as long ago, seeps through the breezed
curtains, light, below the frescoed ceiling
whose winged creatures are echoes waved back—
I do not know whether by mingled or separate

desires of ghosts rising to the lure
of their abandoned places, of my own want
held fast by senses remembering, or by love
prolonged—until the *orangerie,*
the night, and my brain blaze with being.

Clarity Over the Adriatic

Early September in the afternoon
clarity flows from sky to sea to eyes
then again from eyes to sea to sky.

It is as though light-soaked hours
imbue the steel-glazed glare of the sea and—
in time so short that it
is no time at all—
flare into the countless pathways of my brain,
through neurons and synapses that perceive
that glowing brightness, boundless, undefined,
and send no sharp reply. In the same while

the hubbub of the beach draws farther,
colors pale, shapes lose boundaries,
and the body, dispossessed of flesh, is
taken on a backward journey into
the moment when a vast radiance first
appeared, just before space darkened,
matter spun, and time rushed in.

Middlehours, Gulf of Marseilles

From my terrace I hear sounds of middlehours:
nearlight lacing matins on dove beaks,
night doffing blue and stars on seagull wings.

...I follow piney slopes specked with agavé
and yellow thyme, descending to the sea
in opaque morning stillness. The sea returns
brittle surges of spectres, shells
and starfish husks.

Avignon, 1984

Winter goes about reserved in Avignon,
maybe, like me, overwhelmed by mass.
It winds with *Rue Payrollerie*, singing deep
into the sleep of the rocks, deserted,
climbs to the *Place du Palais,* past the Cathedral,
up to the *Rocher de Doms* drooping on the curbing
    Rhône.

A split sky, more restless than the river water,
or the traffic snaking the avenues below the ramparts:
sunset over *la Porte de l'Oulle,* here slivers of rain,
stubborn, unmerciful, gray.

Relic of the wreck, I am the next prey
left at the deepest point of silence of the *Rocher,*
on iron benches edging the pond,
on the farthest line of the balcony,

reaching the shells of a past
that, across the river, seems unchanged:
the Palace of the Kings, *la Tour de Philippe-le-Bel,*
the Abbey, the Manor where we nested, glints of love,
gleams dissolved sooner than consumed.

Exiles

The Indios idol you gave me is on my desk, between
a brass leprechaun and a small Etruscan head,
We visited, moved, talked....When was it?
Poinsettia-leisured afternoons slid on Italian cut
dresses, English bone china in jewelled slender fingers,
uplifted silver spoons and smiles, Ju-Kwa tea pauses,
ripples of colonial thoughts in modulated voices
on child education, Italy going communist, maybe,
France uncertain, England gone socialist, mongolism,
syphilis, Castro, Che Guevara, and Switzerland
so safe and steady like her clocks.

Frozen-daquiri-coolness of jacarandas encased pools
breezed on alabaster and mahogany limbs, mother-of-
        pearl
smiles, buffs of Cologne, Ma Griffe, empanadas, voices
of international banking, affairs, exchanges, deals,
metals, CIA and you smiling and making appropriate
noises in musical scales...

Möet-Chandon galas bubbled under Venetian lanterns
in italianate gardens and on our manicured hands
        glittering,
glittering heirloom rings and baccarat, that clicked
graciously over noises on meat, wheat, Lyndon Johnson,
Nikita Krushchev, the bourse, revolution, torture,
mistresses, and you always resplendent, always serene
gliding along your arpeggio laugh...

43

Now we are gone. Grayness
has set in with grass and lizards. The night air
plays darker music, and lanterns toss mysterious
glares on exotic disorder. Other people speak
of the same things—only the names have changed.

It has happened before, scattered paths, strange roads
to stranger havens. Of all that, some jewels and teacups
have turned up in pawn shops, collector cupboards,
jeweller's windows. Your grandmother's jewelled egg,
its golden heart a minute bird,
now sorrows for passing glances
in some aseptic museum.

The speech of things! and their craving for existence!
Things solving enigmas, things familiar, expansive,
urgent, pressing their holders, welding ceaselessly,
like damned blacksmiths, distance to distance, link
after link...and you, how did you bear up
in foreign traffic?

Landscape

There is a yellower fervor
on the downturned face of sunflowers
as if the yearn to be light spent
still held some bright links of a chain
a source of darkness from below
has begun to snap.

The red language of poppies
is dead in nicotiana fields.
Torrent tales are narrowed
to mumble of mud thread.
Something has cleft the memory of stones,
clipped the wind's whistle.
A new crave wets the bifid tongue
of adders as pale dawn fills
the blank sockets of sugarmills.

There is a bronze child,
his back streaked with oxide,
riding a bronze dolphin,
leaping across the plain
to the delta, to the sea.

Evening-Time Collage

Here is the daylight
slowly sliding down
among timid cyclamens
transparent tides
and blush of fallen leaves

Here is the twilight
leisurely rising like a mobile dome
over the impatient city
surrendering to silence.

Mystical time laden with gentle hues
longed for by souls of vesper
who will hold them in their hand
like magical charms, to soothe
the sorrow of noon.

A resting time for persistent
scientific minds,
entrusting their weariness,
asking for a pause
in the vortex of worlds.

Cocktail time and news time
for business men and aging souls
to break the tight coherence
of the afternoon.

Here is the secret time, creeping
into the abyss between skyscrapers
beneath lowered blinds,
in the cracks of high fences,
of highway bars
beckoning love-seekers and criminals.

Time for sun-hating demons
that soon will roar through mazes
to grip the night's stillness
by the throat.

Inward time for poets
who will grasp the change
and steal nuances
to nurture impatient metaphors
and fill surrounding emptiness.

Entering a Sunken Garden

After a day-long airline strike in Milan,
hours of airport tedium in Heathrow,
lost luggage in New York, I find the garden
waiting as a mother, arms sretched out,
a fragrant haven of herbs and flowers.

As I climb down five steps, bright colors billow,
floating in silence up from a sultry floor.
Late July cuts mosaics in salvia-edged
flowerbeds and tiled paths glow verdigris.

My quick moods slacken through smooth balms that snap
like mountain brackens and lead to a deep corner
where a wrought-iron bench rests, and a whole world
nests forever, where I sit and nearly
whelm in memories of other summers that
eddy in shadow, and the garden stretches
and argues against my wanderlust.

Lights at Romsdal

Day. The bus glides along the Trolls' Road
as through the sequence of a dream.
Stream after stream, U-shaped valleys,
glacial lakes, ice-evened mountains, sated
in argentine light, have left delight
and turbulence fluid in my mind. Now,
rocks that bear the names of pawns—King,
Bishop, Queen—seem beneficent deities
bathed in silver showering from heaven,
and I feel a pigmy in primal awe
before a game of beauty among old giants.

This is as one dreams beauty to be. The mind
aches to find new words to render the changes
lily-light brings to air, mountains water;
but all senses succumb, alert yet dumbstruck
to a speechless siege, until my eyes blink pain.
There is too much brightness to bear
as if the air, bare peaks and waterfalls
cried for it and an incontinent god
complied. Then the unquiet star-mark
implanted in my heart senses violence
and dark shadows striking through that light.

Night. In the underground place
beyond the root of my closed eyes,
ice-green-blue lake after ice-green-blue
lake, holding within their clear surface
the mountains and sourceless lakes
of the sky, flash and shake me awake.
Out of the window I hang awhile between Bishop
and Queen, seeking the propitious signs
men unconsciously plead for.

Even before my soul reaches
for the strength rocks seem to possess
against the force of wind and ice,
silver lights that flow, pitiless,
below, catch and make me touch
the cold frailty of stone, and I know
I am a watcher and a pawn in a lingering
game of passing things, in the hand
of a grave player who ponders his next move.

"Not Blue Roses..."

Someone whispers "Not blue roses..."
to me at this garden party
in April-Washington, D.C., between catkins
at eye level and a blue-roses-steeped hat,
while the lady wearing it
recounts her trans-Siberian trip.

Once someone said to me:
"Not a German blue"
of his impossible blue eyes.
It was as if the sky had put on
a new light-skin to give away the secret
of his face, to let the golden catkins,
dangling in that blue, shine a short while
longer between dwarf hill and dwarf hill
where he was found drifting.

We never knew the full story
of his trek from Siberia
to the Apennine sniper-shot.
He had not enough language to tell us
about twenty-two years of his life
in a thirty-minute reprieve
before catkins tumbled and blue skies
sank in his and millions of eyes.

I repeat "Not blue roses" and mean:
I will not grab the lady's hat.
She may finish her story, as if to say
"Not + a + name + color" makes a life, a story secure.
To have said "Not a German blue"; "Not a Jew blue";
"Not a Russian blue"; "Not anybody's blue,"
and all catkins fall naturally.

The lady did not like her journey,
"...not a decent cup of coffee..."
Hang on, don't fall on me, catkin,
or I'll let out that all-color scream
checked in my throat.

Quarrel with Death

Sunset

There is a confusion of signs
in day's reluctance to decline;
a fervor shifts from tangerine
to green, to gray, as if light
desired to leave a perfect pattern.

So my brain, to slow the pill-charted
path of pain, moves to create
shining architectures of escape
—petals falling to the ground
raise airy castles on waterlily ponds;
a stranger's smile on a street casts
a flight of wings that clear
my restless sky.

My diminishing universe, about to yield
to an all-consuming shine of black, traces,
brilliantly, the cry of my expectant flesh
in a furl of morning-glories.

I have come to love this space of grace
between the burning and the blossoming
of pain, as the poet loves the idea
before it shapes into words.

Insomnia

The purple bulls of night
have raped time in its ash cave.

The eyes claim darkness which won't
anoint them with its black oils.

Tides of burbling sounds
lumber through the blank window.

Neon lights spin webs, spindly
moss loose, into the hollow
between the planets' giddy glare.

My desire jolted by high-volted
pylons of your lack comes back
with a cry of loss.

Quicksilver spills over the quivering
anemones of flesh, nailed to a litter

by the talons of a jasmine moon
that wound even the color of darkness.

Transitions
(after T.S. Eliot)

The morning rises to upper rooms
smelling of kitchen coffee
and golden lights through jalousies,
dazzle, in windy patterns,
walls and eyelids that would hold to sleep.
Newspapers race the doors
with donkey hooves, footsteps rumble
the leafy street.
Yesterday comes back;
the crystals of slumber crack.
I slide, reluctant, to the edge of the bed,
dangle legs and feet
that tap the floor for slippers.
Turning the knob of the bathroom door,
I think of others who, like me,
caught in a trudging pantomime,
perform the same and lonely acts.
I don my mask.

Beneath the high arcades, along the curbs,
as evening slants across the passersby,
towers, pillars, trees
trail longer shadows on the pavings.
My eyes are sunk in a dying sky
above the building's zebra glass;
and those who spent the afternoon
in city parks
are gone like pigeons struck by bells.
The town thickens with silence, dark things.

My bargains with the night begin
at twelve o'clock.
In the thick space of the bed,
with sleep half-traded in my arms,
my naked face dissolves
into the dark swell of dreaming.

Night Over Gibraltar

The ocean seems to snore quietly on the shore,
the lewd monkeys are asleep. The Rock, stiff
as an ancient priest, presides over starsilence
propitiating shapes of night—the levigated
stillness rising from the swimming-pool, like
an expanse from another world; the sword thrust
of agavé spikes; the webs of eucalyptus and
fig trees; the perilous glow of pomegranate.

In a time like this one may think to have grown
used to anything—the mailbox swelling
mostly with junk mail; at diminishing intervals
some envelope bordered with a blank band;
dimness; journeying alone; phone rarely
ringing. One may try to ignore the nearly
unbearable squeaks of the irondoor ward
at the unsteady turning of the key, and
the mind's distress at not knowing what
awaits beyond the iron portal until one's eyes
fall casually on the mouth of the ocean open wide.

Ravenna, 1985

It was here where the land was haloed
with Byzantine gold, where Romanesque towers
bridged earth to sky, that sunset stirred
its sarabands on the white ledge of sands.

Evening wore slowly, streaking with dark
the sandroses on the dunes, leaning low
on the stretched-forth necks of horses,
slowing their homebound urgency.

The air offered, then, an ancient pity,
a pledge of salvation for youth's uncertainties,
a prayer could open a heart.
Now the leaden sea hurls rubbish

on concrete shores; the horses have been
evicted and the sandroses starve
beneath barbed wires. In day-dissolving hours
gray furies of refineries heave up

their clouds of red nightmares. The night
once starred and calm consumes itself
anonymous and vague like God's face
on the parched wall of a chapel.

Prison Night

On the electric wires white doves
woo the terrace tiles;
the stable paws the ground
yearning for night hunts.
Jasmines spring silver claws
to tear the eyes.

Moon bars plunge landward. Where
are the sandbanks, the
compassion of shadows, the flow
of sleep? For two weeks
there has been a hindering halo
all dark long, a pursuing song
of madness dispiriting the stars.

I have sought to make myself a lane
along the night to a safe lookout,
but my thoughts spread and shift
like flocks of moths ensnared
by rims of dark. The frost-stark
manacles of the moon are too strong
for the slender essence of my mind.

Telephone Call, 3 a.m.

Keen teeth,
his words
bite my eardrums,
shark tails
flap on my brain.

Drops of eclipse
from the eaves of the moon,
yesterday
bleeds in its hollow.

Seas of stars
over my head,
ashes below my feet,
the night shivers
at my window.

Ice cubes click
in the pool of night,
cymbals and violins
have taken flight
from his memory.

Alcohol metaphors
on the wires,
that voice
an ancient dying....

Requiem

Clouds blindfold the night,
black miles are running.

She drives her car,
the radio is playing.

On a curve of the highway
madness is preying.

A police car slides along,
his face is grinning.

Darkness pools her cries,
fury is spinning.

Winds do not blow
where her body is lying.

Trees do not care,
stones are not crying.

A shadow stalks the night.
Black miles are running.

As Rain the Flesh

The sudden thought of you
surprises me, as rain the flesh
on a hot day when the eyes
surmise the hue
the wet landscape will take.
Sense awakened, yet at rest
like a high nimbus, unwavering,
a steady sheen livened by light.
Short stream of peace
earth after rainfall
but the sky is full
of swift changes,
brief fragile things.
Someone stood at door-dark waving,
and red, dewed poppyflowers wavered.

On the Shoulder of the Westward Wind

There is a great darkening-out
that circles the world
once seemingly domestic now engaged
in tearing the gold fabric of the mind.

There is a song droned in a foreign tongue
on the shoulder of the westward wind
between lights that no longer change,
no longer lure to calm bewilderment.

There is a mourning sound from death's room
roaming round and round
until it reaches the place it came from,
leaving no more than formless quivers,
traces of ashes on fingertips.

Fish

What lightning and the rain
confide to the waves is ever a secret
I am another fish, sunk light-deep,
under the brunt of a harder current
that pulls me upstream
to yet another sea that keeps
itself as yet indistinct.
The water-skin and ferns flinch
and shrivel underfin. I slip by,
my gills filled by a vague desire,
that has not yet found a name.

Long Distance

Hallo! Hallo! You mean God?
Oh, pardon me! I thought you did not exist.
Very gracious of you to forgive...What?
A whole series? So the Hindus guessed right
about your program of repeats.
Would I subscribe to it? I don't think
I truly can. Did I not like the preview?
It isn't that...the stage choreography
was beautiful, I'd say superb. The actors?
Well, let me tell you. I had a small part
in the chorus...we were a sorry lot all along.
The presence of a stage director or producer
might have helped. Did you say the script?
As for that, a translation in my native language
would have been essential for understanding, you know.
A repeat performance? No, I am sorry, I could not,
honestly I could not go through all that again.
No, I do not contradict myself. What an agony
it would be...a leading role? Impossible, sir.
Yes, I understand it would help you too. I know
about the crisis, but the idea of not being able
to argue some controversial passages in the script
scares me...What? You can't change it? Oh God...

Sure Thing

I do not know what the end
of all this will be.
Whether in a PUFF
or UHM, sweet or sour,
cold or hot.

The sure thing is that
there will be nobody
here to remember, though we,
poor mongrels, have worked
so hard for immortality.

What Will Happen to You?

You grasped my hand, gasped "Don't let me die."
since then I've tried to make you live the only way
I could. I used spaces, objects that outlasted you
as God, clay for an act of creation. I said the word—
your name—in my Eden, your study, kept untouched,
and you walked out of your secret space, the unlit
face of the moon on the clock dial, like a chastised
child eager to leave his punishment corner.
For ten years we celebrated our rites of life there,
and night dissolved over the closeness of our bodies.

I cannot remember when spindrift began to blow,
and blur things and your image before my eyes.
I did not let you go. I used what other four senses
remembered, touched the tortoise paperweight on the
        desk,
and felt the seaweed coolness of your hands; smelled
your pipe, the scent of you lingering in the air;
ate your favorite candies; played your song over and over
to dispel that pervading dull-bright whiteness.

Today I feel the spindrift, changed to thick foam,
inch along all channels of my body. What is left
of senses is scarily diminishing. I have to bend
my head a few inches away from your picture album.
Objects are colder and colder to the touch; scent,
a faint trace; candies, bitter; your song, the tic tac
of the clock, a hiss, or at best a buzz. A world,
ours, is receding to a point and I can't help.
Even the pages of memory turn backward, more
        uncertain,
opaque by the hour, portending pure evanescence at the
        end.

I imagine how you would be now, what lines
would have changed your face, what thoughts, what tone
of voice you might have if you spoke. The camera of the
        mind
spits out single snapshots, nearly black, stilled in instants
that never flow, and I ask myself what will happen to you
when the moon-face dial has no more hours.

Miserere

Miserere

Hours of hills, barren ravines,
chancy tablelands run behind bodies
like springs wrung, and released by flight.
Breath beats the heart on shell-shocked leaves,
any beat last-ticking. Feet crash undergrowth.
Hands, clutching weapons, push aside
anything lying in the corrupted woods.
Pupils dilated by faces of death
telescope fragments of sky,
scarlet announcements of dark.

Miserere for the foe, ally decades ago.

****

Hours of hills behind, bodies tense
and relax in pursuit. Hands grip weapons,
hold steering wheels, adjust sights
over the hills ahead. Feet tread trails
the enemy has trod.
Death-filled eyes probe clearings,
scan the same sky
for comforting signs of night.

Miserere for the ally, our future enemy.

****

Night, be dark over the shaken hills.
Hills, be cave-scooped, steep-walled.
Cloud-capped, hide shadow-casting moons.
The parsley flower and rosemary wither.
Glowworms dim on your scorched skin.

Miserere for those who will not see dawn.

****

Lower all flags. They fly colors of death.
In eerie wind they swirl and spin and twist
the insane blazon on Cain.

Miserere for the mother who will curse her womb.

****

Bards, cover your mouths. Take a good look.
We do not die for glory. Where we are going
even glory rots. Hear the screams jetting forth.
See the blood clotted by terror, cratered hearts,
charred flesh, gushing entrails, the anguished masks
fleeting before darkness sucks us in.

Miserere, miserere for all herds driven to stockyards.

Mine-field — 1946

Horns of black bulls
on the rim of the sun.
Shadows of crows
fly left
through sulfur skies.
The ace of spades
turned upside down.

Within dark steel seeds
a blind core ticks,
waits in rows
under the sleepless
vipers of the grass.

A ball, heavy with cold air
and raven breath, moves
along the path
of broken columns.

Where are you going, child,
with your hands
full of wind and
feet full of wings?

Sweet oleander
of an unlucky womb,
black wind-splinters
ripped you away,
long tongues of purple flames
charred your petals.

Sweet oleander
of the parched night,
the half-closed door
of your mother's house
is draped by hearts
burned black
and the foam
of crystal tears.

Sing a Lullaby

A wreck of World War I, father
died in nineteen twenty-one.
Slender the years Mother's
warmth lulled my fears. Brief
the inviting smile, the teasing
glare of young girls that beheld
wonders, dreams we would never share.

Sudden trumpets of war dulled
all feelings and the songs of summer.
Mothers, fathers, friends, girls
put on their goodbye hands,
waving the tune of military bands.
The world's clocks struck midnight,
then the arms started and kept whirling.
Flowers of minds just barely budded.

I hardly felt the bullet's bite and kiss.
My last sight blurred on a yellow broom;
my blood emptied into this unlapping creek,
a red water moon drowned my dreams.
Life, motion, light floated downstream
toward where all shortened lives, drop
by drop, leak their parting grief.

For me, companions, just a lullaby —
if you are here tomorrow.

Orders: Don't Let Him See Your Shadow

As a hound smells the hunted hare
I smelled your presence through meadows,
ridges, thickets, orchards, groves.

I got to know your shape, your back,
your gait. I traced the motion
of your hands like the roadmaps
of the mountains where we fought.

You did not know I saw through you
as through the streams that greened
the woods that sheltered us, nor that I
shared your hours, habits, space,
the sky you breathed.

Persistents as a lover, I
pursued, and assembled
the shady puzzle of your acts.

You hardly heard or knew.
Fury, anguish, orders drummed my blood
as I discharged them all on you,
informer, with my gun.

In Memory of Roberto Tinti, Called Bob, Commander of the 34th Garibaldi Brigade

You ducked, shouted,
"Damn you, get down!"
and tucked me in your arms,
strong, gentle as a mother
at bedtime.

A mother's gesture flutters on this air
dark as the wine we drank
in our village pub on the lighter side
of our red moon.

Drops of red moonlight on your handkerchief,
at dusk coming and your nightfall.
"Peace," you said when I visited you last,
"is like being dead." You seemed misplaced in peace:
locust, lawyer, jackal followed the condor—
and the lion.

Silence had followed you, as you stared at
and measured the shortest distance
between plain and hill
where the many lives you led to battle fell,
leaves not yet sapped into fullness.

Will you, will they
hear the full mourning of my bugle
crying that distance now,
peaking where slopes are steepest,
whining where fogs tighten
the lowland where you lie?

Other graves grow at the lowland's edge.
from distant ledges honeysuckle comes,
and honeysuckle hedges are thickest.
It is not difficult to find these hedges;
scent offers an easy lane to follow.

I follow the scent, sit here
within the still walls of white two-lipped flowers.
As long as I suck from their calyx
you will taste honey, bleed your black smile.

In lightfall, long in fainting,
someone behind touches my arm,
asks: "And you are you, here, weeping?"
I do not know him; he is young,
but he knows this place.

Out of Bounds

Tonight the city, weary, still as a dead insect
webbed in narrow-winding streets, has fallen
finally to sleep. The streetlamp, pale as evening
yeast, haloes the "Out-of-bound" sign scrawled by the
victor's hand on the walls of the fog-shrouded alley.

Here lines of Hitler's last resort, boys in gray
uniforms, close-packed with loneliness, bartered
fears with sharp jokes whose brush strokes blended
Baltic-June beaches with December-latin plains.
They waited, spider-patient, for
bandy bodies of girls
they would pick up in the red parlor for a few
packages of cigarettes, or a can of lard.

No certainties, here, within the gray grip
of defeated sky, but the persistent beat
in the blood, lewd needles in the groin,
the swivel of snakes mounting from the pit
of the stomach to the throat, and in the ears
the somewhere-north nostalgic sound of harmonica
buried in the brain with the half-recalled
smile of a golden girl, leaning from a haystack,
and the mild fever of not yet despair
in the mother's caressing hands.

There, back in the blind alley, where
on his way out, a boy's stalked life was taken,
the final beats of *Heimat, Heimat* flew
from his no longer human fist that sticks out,
stiff, from the embrace of a brown blanket.

Purple flower closed before dawn, now
an ember in my mind, that fist emerges
from the bleeding band in the center of the sign—
stands, as if waiting for a stay not granted,
opens palm down and sweeps away the scrawl
like rubbish. The fingers clench again, except
the accusing one, that writes "Pity on the living"
in the neat handwriting of the dead.

Someone had laid a scarlet carnation, then,
where desire had flaked off. Bell beats would
later break the bounds of life beyond the Alps:
a girl's smile would go limp, a mother lift
a fist of tears in the empty room.

War Village

Only snow moves. Silence oozes
—a chill film on bits of windowglass.
No use looking for half-buried bodies, lips,
ears, eyes, in this forsaken simulacrum
of a place—the battered trunk of main street
decays into scourged downs, disfigured woods,
the old heart stumbled into the arms
of the eyeless Tax Collector claiming
total tribute on the church square.

"I shall claim no name"—the maimed Saint,
standing upon the sky-vaulted altar, seems to say:
"I shall claim no name, for myself, for the
village, for its people, wasted on uncaring
masters. The poor never knew the reason
for their last stand, nor why
fearful verses mumbled in their blood
at the iron prompting of the gun.
They clung to mud houses, crumbs,
the old ways, carrying the outdated weapons
of their mind, loaded partly with movements
of seasons, partly with movements
between cemetery and church. Be gone!
Enemies or friends, you are strangers
to this place, its past, its no-future.
Rust has seized the plough blade,
rot has wedged in the sharpening stone.

Be gone. My bones will lie
peacefully beneath the crudely chiselled
stone from which my name was gone
long before the villagers ceased to say it.''

The snow-lit figure, the church are left
alone with silence and its secrets.
Shadows, bent double, face a cruel wind
sounding them as they flick down the slope
beside scarred chestnuts, singed oaks. The last
scavenger presence gone, everything begins
to turn pure, pristine. Over the hill the maimed
Saint's arm stabs out—a silver dagger.

August Night in the Emilian Lowlands

Poplars of fireflies
and falling stars
crown Etruscan canals
and ambush the silence.

Willows of witchcraft
and watermagic trace
Roman land-divisions
over Gallic defeat.

Silky Chinese foam
rises on mulberry leaves
and the moon grows richer
with white fruits
in the obsidian night.

In Byzantine cloisters,
moonridden, stray dogs
wail the sorrow
of the absent Jews.

An immense poppy closes,
bonfires burn
on multiple horizons.

Within flatland cages
of canes and dry-wheat breezes,
cicadas, nightingales and toads
scythe their sickle-songs
and harvest the spikes of silence.

This Sunday Long Ago

At dusk the Sforza Palace is a drowsing dinosaur
sprawled outside my window. Milan, deserted,
sleeps off the boredom of the afternoon—this Sunday
      long ago.
Duskfall on the curfewed streets. Drizzle
mists the half moon windows of the cellar room.

Inside, our shadows move about a printing press.
You hand me a sheet of paper, speaking to us all:
"For God's sake, use words our readers understand.
What do they know of pacifism?" "All right,"
I grumble, "give us ten minutes."

Ten minutes and bootfalls trample the courtyard's
marble slabs, one downflight of stairs. Deputies
of lunatic gods push us and you through the turbid gulf
of their long night, past your mirage of palms
and olive groves. Now you live gilt and glorified

like an early Christian legend in the mosaics
and rock paintings of our minds. Today, loose
in the Rose of Winds, prophets with white eyes
speak in sibyl words, and we are forsaken

in the swift reversal of language. Old sinister
meanings creep into speech, break the visions
and images of the spirit. The envoy's message
is betrayed at its very enunciation. Christian
non-Christian brawls burst like fumaroles.

Did you die for nothing? Could you return
among us, would your story be changed? You see,
here, like the small mammals of millenia ago,
only the shrewd survived. It is late. The drizzle
trickles down the windowpane, gathers on the sill,
pools on darkened streets. Should that mysterious
force in which you believed, which binds contraries
together, descend again upon the living, would it flow
from Galilee to Teheran, to Milan,
then come flooding back?

Po Valley

Those plains,
where evening entered summer gardens
crowded with grandmother chatter,
click of teacups, children's tinfoil sabers,

where silence grappled with cicada drone
on distant pastureland, and on the church square
belltolls hurled and tossed
pigeons to flight—

so there I sat on the wide windowseat
of evening, and watched it create
imperishable things,
like those globetrotter tales
the smoke from the farmhouse chimney rewrote
on the mutable-cloud sky
above the maniac castle, the calm courtyards,
in wide eyes of old men and star children.
I breathed the winey breath of evening
from the pub, the bursting brambleberry bush.
So I saw the spunsugar gypsy evening
at Saturday fairs clap its laborious sales
in stacking of many hands.

So why, even then, that taste of a death coin
under the tongue, that overhanging sense of loss—
grapes grown in shade,
two or three berries falling unripened?

So now the no-sound of evening coming from plains of
   graves,
and the raising and pounding of a cross
on my hearth's hill.

Auschwitz Revisited

I am here because of a synecdoche of the heart.
One of the figures of love passed to me
by your brother, who, poet and sole survivor
of your family, started the search for you.
The few marks, given to us by one who saw
you taken from the convoy, scant, nearly
unreadable, were swiftly filled as those of hares
beneath an incorporeal dance of snow,
and the search grew wearily into pilgrimage.
For years, in the long alliance between Scroll
and Rose, your brother, my grandparents and I
visited the sites we imagined contained you.

When pain tightened around our throats
or the awareness of the loss, bent like a bow
to the farthest point of tension, released
its arrows, you emerged from the wreckage
of your people and mine
—out of the shade of willows and sycamores
you sat again the night with me on the cathedral steps,
our thoughts filling the L-shaped square like lamplight;
at Christmas dinners you came into being, gulping down
with gusto the pudding of grandmother's cook:
"Sinfully, sinfully delicious."
At concerts it was you playing the organ at mass
in my family's chapel. From the pit of baroque
Synagogues you winked up at me, a Christian girl,
curious and indignant at her exile in the matroneum.

How many times the four of us heard your laughter
roving through the silver palms of a procession,
your message of peace superimposed to song.

In all these years you have been shrinking out of reach;
your coming and going fused with that of the other
     three
who are also gone. What remains is a pressure
a longing in the breast, scar tissue of a deep wound
that could burst and bleed at any time.
You have taken to incarnating in a blinding flash,
then disappearing, leaving a wave of thought,
a shadow of a shape by the eyes.

Today, in this place, in a puff of smoke
or icy breath of air, I do not know whether it is
your whisper or mine: "Keep your wits, my girl,
try to keep them among the insane."
I've tried, Conrad, I've tried, but it's difficult.
As difficult as still looking for your glasses,
and seeing this huge collective glare
implacably stare through my groping fingers;
or walking this bone-dust softly softly
so as not to step on you.

Diaspora for John Pauker

Your voice is like a wooden pipe lamenting,
so far away from the Hungarian brome,
so far away, and sadness left remaining
like a body flung off, naked, to the winds.

Song of a Mother to Her Child

My youth ran awry in scorching trails of war.
In time for thought and of love-blooming age
when only wonders stirred about the curious mind,
my world was crossed by hot streams of blood,
and flesh and dust were my only code.

Between the desperate portent of the womb
and my touching of your tender flesh
to my hearing of your first cry of hunger,
a past of violence and nothing was left
by stony voices of the dead.

Pain taught me the verbs of life,
love linked in secret with my wrath.
In double bondage, how to speak of past?
What voice could my milk spew out
but that of madness and deceit?

To give my love a shape and show you love
I could use only the gestures of a mime—
my movements, pliant pirouettes, a game
to teach you to avoid the raging traffic;
the vignettes my hands clumsily sketched,

a touch to ease the raw edges of our page;
the smirks of my pale painted face, mere tricks
to elicit laughter that may delay the dull
single tone of the drone pipe of darkness.

Frankfurt am Main

Hereditary friendship, a brotherhood that held through
iron times, differences, adversity. Each year, since the end
of World War II, like two knight loyal to an old ritual,
one of us reached the other across the Atlantic. Thus we
    failed
to see what four decades had done to us. This chilly winter
    of
1984, it is my turn to visit. Hans, lars and butler of the
household, had warned me, gently, at the airport: "His
    mind
is vague at times..."

As I approach the tall figure coming toward me, the usual
pleasant pang contracts my stomach: same stare—deep
    sunken
blue—, straight nose, elegance in gesturing. Heinrich
    bends
in the habit of handkissing; words in German-slightly-
    accented
French tease my ears: "Toujours ravissante..." and I:
    Heinrich,
you old liar, let me kiss you! He smiles, a childish smile,
I think. Yet at a closer scrutiny I see something has
    beclouded
the old radiance.

Later in the library, poised on Biedermeier chairs, sipping
Negroni, we let drip out year-long news. The stained glass
light creates cadences of illusion, the classic features of
his face assume youthful tightness and mirth as he informs
    me
he HAD to invite his new neighbors for dinner the next
    day.
"One has to cope with newness...Don't we know?"

Then some delicate vapors condense on the skin of silence.
His mind disperses in bivouacs of victory and defeat. A
    stare
empty as the eyefall of a Greek statue ebbs from me to
    fireplace
to walls. He and his house sigh, one world collapses
    inward.
I whisper a strangled plea: "Darling, come back."
    Immobile
he replies: "They are late...They ought to know how
    lateness
upsets me..."

Two paintings on the wall at my left side: his brother and
sister—Ulla and Friedrich—at eighteen. He, lost in
  Russia,
she, identified by the engraving on her wedding ring. I
  dare
not think of all other busts, miniatures, portraits, and dust
souls scrabbled through centuries on Earth. I concentrate
  on
the vellum of this home, illuminated by the absurdity of its
living and dead. Expanding from pictorial calm, sorrow
  makes
his face a tragic mask. The drink tastes hemlock. I am
  saved
by Hans announcing dinner. A tender pressure on his
  master's
shoulder prompts a shiver: "Have I dozed off? How
  awful...
the drink perhaps..." I keep up the pretense, smiling and
denying.

For three hours the permanence of grace and strict
  adherence
to form—long become substance—hold against the
  encroachment
of ghosts. Heinrich is Heinrich again, witty and amusing.
A fair and happy evening, but for Requiems on his piano
  keyboards,
and an old man's hand helping me up the stairs.

Next morning after breakfast, we take a walk down the
    garden,
past the folly, to the deserted banks of the Main, airily
patterned by ice. Heinrich's mood, somber as his
    Northern
sky, his voice gravely recycling the unadorned past, reveal
a melancholy man reduced to mathematical rigor by a
    brain that
does and does not forget. His pain, supersaturated,
    explodes
at the softest touch: "I am a soldier, I was...too long a
    nightmare
all along...all my beloved gone...I am a human being..."
I offer my garbled consolation: "Darling, it takes
    centuries
to decant the sediment of mankind. It is a matter of
    distance.
Who by now speaks with rage about the Chaldeans, Nero,
    or Gengis
Khan?" Suddenly, struck by a bolt of absurdity, I fall
    silent.
All I can do is extend my arthritic hand to grasp the
    thread-bare
limit of his loneliness.

So much lack of mercy. Will hate ever evaporate, and, like
the tears running to my mouth, leave no other sediment
    than
a faintly bitter aftertaste of salt?

At the Edge of the Land

Rain

Memories and rain
open the day.
Incidents fall
and ripple
the path of morning
and afternoon.
Only one sound,
the sound of rainfall—
a voice that cannot be deciphered,
a voice with no questions
and no answers.
By evening,
the day has rained itself
away,
as always.

Spring, 1982

What made the sun hide
in crevices this April?
A few ants, bark-brown, loose-jointed
creep over the window sill,
walk over the steel sink, emigrate
to the breakfast table to tell me
to prepare for spring.

Look at my quilted robe
crawl over my cold bones. Hear my cough.
In the garden crocuses are crystals,
the daffodils are baffled and look down
as if to marvel at snow.

Spring indeed. I brush away the nearest ant.
It falls to the kitchen floor, lands gracefully,
and, like a hurried acrobat, disappears
under the carpet. Another takes its place
on the rim of my white and blue plate
to summon me to an inveterate purpose.

You are growing old—an ant's voice says—
you forget how to read signs.
Baffled or not the daffodils are here
and so are we. The sun is at the door.

Confluence
(for Bosa de Franceski)

Someone, I have forgotten who,
used to say we make friends
only in childhood, Bosa,
and I thought so too, till our Sunday
afternoon stroll along the Sava,
that carried faraway tales and
suggestions of spring into the Danube.
The unique times of two women,
no matter how middle-aged, an intimate
confluence. Like the rivers, Bosa,
we travel great distances,
nothing too short or too long for our course.
Our religion is the law of flowing,
our temptation is the plain, our sin is
outflowing, our redemption receding,
our interdict the rock, our passion the sea.
We keep flowing forth, in times of great clouds
or terse skies,
cleaving and filling space,
mindless of unsteady earth below, of men's tales,
and surreal time-space, searching
for affinity, which is the confluence
of elements composing and composed...

At the frown of the land we wash,
we wash the brown salt on the banks
with spiced waters, feeding
rosemary, myrtle and linden,
leaving scented driftwood
at the gates of men's cities.
We are women of a new fauna,
not guilty or innocent,
outside the Bible and the Koran,
women of ourselves, nobody else's.
The sum of our flowing has come together
in the same breath of wind
carrying whiffs of emerald sea salts...
We are ready for the taste.
Our faces are not made up and wear no mask,
our hands still grip the scimitar
of the moon over low-flying birds of prey.

I Shall Be There

I shall be there
instead of brooding in my room.
I will wait in winter weather for the D4,
at 30th and Q, within the deadly
invisible ooze of chemical and monoxide.

I shall be there,
holding my unfinished poem to my breast,
through the malevolent traffic of D.C.,
the sickly red hue of Mass. Ave.
Impatient horns will sing moon songs.
The needle-tattooed dregs in DuPont
Circle will don childhood Sunday dress.

I shall be there,
having turned the wretched houses, turgid
with rusty pipes and fire escapes, into abodes
fit for kings; the ugly cement, metal, and glass
beehives into gracious old Regency homes;
pornos into Goodwill stores; restored
healthy trees to the avenues.

I shall be there,
hearing the sirens of the art deco
fountain sing Irish ballads, and the dolphins
articulate uncoded alphabets. Public libraries
are open and children queue to enter:
white and black poets are reading.

I shall be there,
knocking at the door. "Knock hard"
the sign reads. I will climb the steep
stairway and be encircled by my friends.

I shall be there:
Over a cup of wine or herbal tea, memories
glow like fireflies in August nights; proper
mots flower interspersed with raisins
and sunflower seeds. Care is the rarest
orchid on the trellis of our terrace.

I shall be there
to see words, grammar, syntax take
golden sabers and make strange right
from wrong. Dictators drown in tea cups,
cabalas repair the troubled world. Tired
spirits soar to undiscovered galaxies.

I shall be there
and leave drunk of you: Shirley,
Jean, Mary Ann, Gabriele, Judy,
and Carolyn. Then back in my room,
like a satisfied bloodsucker,
I shall explode with poetry.

Black Cemetery in Georgetown
*(for Dr. Lee Eiden who on a misty day's stroll
gave me the idea of "a graveyard of a graveyard")*

The trees here float with winter mists,
ghosts strolling on soft shores.
Here, like is known by like
and contemplation is the contemplated.

A swollen river overflows.
Here, the past spills over into the future and,
retreating, leaves the landscape changed.
Heaviness may levitate in mats
of gossamer, and veer to liquid syllables.
Mist, names, and gravestones meld
till they are one.

Read names on upright stones,
names that should have bloomed
like any flower in any season.
Instead, flowers bloom inward,
become the unintelligible change.

Within this shapeless graveyard
of a graveyard other somber changes
creep with larvae beneath the shell
of earth. Shorter than our dreams,
the images of death will live less than letters
chiseled on our fallen stones.

Even future quiescence is denied us.
We are not allowed to rest
in the calm prison of the trees;
nor the leaves, wise with what lies
between the wind and absence of wind, are left
to draw the light, to us forbidden.

At the gate bulldozers wait to drag
marble, trees, earth and bones
to another stifling night.
A whiff of fog, perhaps
our last fighting breath,
will trespass over Oak Hill's
metal fences, to recall our alikeness,
the center of design
where spheres, opposites, and rules
come to their point of winter.

Melpomene: the Singing One

Listen to that sharp note.
It repeats between two hidden surfaces,
then waves away over the sky willows—
a resigned murmur
washing-back.

Listen. Any other sound that hesitates
is incidental and lost
to the mesh of echoes that float
on the breath of seasons, yet remain—
until all tones of a mysterious
scale are exhausted.

Late Afternoon

Tired, we drive
through sluggish winter void.
Beneath the steady scansion of the wheels
edgeless roads follow fields
to infinite half-light.

Vast, past hours clot
the space between us.
Each tuft of reed holds,
like a prelude,
echoes of solitude.

You take my hand. Palms press. Fingers
interlock, as if praying for mercy
like the builders of dikes and wharves
beyond *Les Saintes-Maries*
already behind us.

Through the windshield, grey
with dust and dead insects,
night appraises the ending day,
traces a graph of colors, shadows, shapes
spelling last time, nothing more.

We cannot reclaim the ancient trails of the *Camargue* we
    walked on,
nor the lookout posts, cabins and custom house,
the inconstant Rhône lost
to the legislation of the sea.

Our evening is like this:
we have anticipated
that our lanes will separate.
Before light withdraws we would like to say
unforgettable words.

"Je m'appelle..."

The music box has lost its voice
The worn-out gears are blocked.
A cross-gesture in the air, the figurine
stands, unaware of the lack of sound,
unaware of the fixed pin that once
linked it to motion. Will the spin
and song, which are now stilled,
begin again elsewhere, here?

Somewhere you too have revolved
pinned to the axle of your gear
moving concordant with the gears of day,
night and sound. You have watched
their pitchlines coalesce with your pitchline—
white growing out of black, black out of white,
sound out of silence, silence out of sound.
Vaguely, when conscious, you have sensed
no contradiction: that was no foreign space,
just a space altered, to which something was
constantly added and removed.

Now circles are restlessly widened and a sing-song
is heightened by a faster turning—grandfather's
minah-bird's last words: "Je m'appelle
François, pauvre François!"

114

You are taken by surprise by the gear's
friction and the pitchlines' stillness.
You do not know yet that the minah-bird's
voice has gone inside your center, with black,
white, song, and dance and all is but the echo
of your voice: "Je m'appelle…"

"See Me,"

see me, and let us touch
for once. I am in a Now
which memory mingles
to a Then when
I saw the sky clear and open,
day sun-deep,
night wear no other garment
than moon or star lace,
no barrier blacken out
my vision of the cliff-lines.
Do not thrust away
my clumsy reach this time.
O let me touch you
for once because now
is when I say loudly—
"I have loved you,
mothers, fathers, children
of the world, I love you all.
I speak the terrible language
of falling stars. Hear it,
quickly. The cliffs
are plummeting into us."

Scripta humanistica

Directed by
BRUNO M. DAMIANI
The Catholic University of America
COMPREHENSIVE LIST OF PUBLICATIONS *

- Juan de Mena, *Coplas de los siete pecados mortales: Second and Third Continuations.* Ed. Gladys Rivera. $25.50
- Salvatore Calomino, *From Verse to Prose: The Barlaam and Josaphat Legend in Fifteenth-Century Germany.* $28.00
- Darlene Lorenz-González, *A Phonemic Description of the Andalusian Dialect Spoken in Almogía, Málaga — Spain.* $25.00
- Maricel Presilla, *The Politics of Death in the «Cantigas de Santa María.»* Preface by John E. Keller. Introduction by Norman F. Cantor. $27.50
- *Studies in Honor of Elias Rivers,* eds. Bruno M. Damiani and Ruth El Saffar. $25.00
- Godwin Okebaram Uwah, *Pirandellism and Samuel Beckett's Plays.* $28.00

BOOK ORDERS

* Clothbound. *All book orders,* except library orders, must be prepaid and addressed to **Scripta Humanistica**, 1383 Kersey Lane, Potomac, Maryland 20854. *Manuscripts* to be considered for publication should be sent to the same address.